Sparks of Celtic Mystery

soul poems from Éire

Cheryl Lafferty Eckl

FLYING CRANE PRESS

SPARKS OF CELTIC MYSTERY: SOUL POEMS FROM ÉIRE.
Copyright © 2019 by Cheryl Eckl | Cheryl Lafferty Eckl.
All poems and epigraphs are © 2015-2019.
Except where noted, all images are from the author's personal collection.
All rights reserved. Flying Crane Press, Livingston, Montana 59047
Cheryl@CherylEckl.com | www.CherylEckl.com

Library of Congress Control Number: 2019900557
ISBN: 978-0-9970376-4-7 (pbk.)
ISBN: 978-0-9970376-7-8 (ebk.)

The author wishes to gratefully acknowledge
    Cover and interior design: James Bennett
    Publishing support: Theresa McNicholas

Printed in the United States of America

Sparks of
Celtic Mystery

Books by Cheryl Lafferty Eckl

Poetry

Poetics of Soul & Fire

Bridge to the Otherworld

Idylls from the Garden
of Spiritual Delights & Healing

Sparks of Celtic Mystery:
soul poems from Éire

Prose

A Beautiful Death:
Keeping the Promise of Love

A Beautiful Grief:
Reflections on Letting Go

The LIGHT Process:
Living on the Razor's Edge of Change

The Weaving:
A Novel of Twin Flames Through Time

Contents

For lovers of Celtic mysteries

May the call of Éire
bring a light to your heart,
a song to your soul
and peace to your spirit.

Éire's Call of Home & Soul

Surely it is no wonder if Ireland feels like home to you. Signs proclaiming céad míle fáilte (a hundred thousand welcomes) are everywhere, greeting you like your grandmother's embrace, a home-cooked meal, a warm fire and a cozy bed.

Your first sight of the glistening green landscape begins to calm your mind and heal your jet lag. The exhilarating energy of salty sea air and wild Atlantic waves crashing against massive cliffs invigorates body and soul. The feeling of gentle, grassy earth beneath your feet seems to beckon, "Come, rest awhile and be at peace."

A pot of strong tea served with fresh scones, strawberry jam and butter from the world's most contented cows is sure to soothe even the most jangled travelers. And the fresh, organic produce from local farms will make you want to only eat meals prepared by one of Ireland's masterful chefs.

Yet more than dramatic landscapes, incredible food and genuine hospitality, Ireland exudes the feeling of a place your soul knows, perhaps better than anywhere you've ever been.

Pronounce the island's Gaelic name and you will know what I mean. Éire (ay-rhe) must be voiced out on a gentle breath, tripped softly on the tongue, cradled in the mind and gathered back into the heart as a vow to return once more to somewhere so sacred you dare not speak it harshly or in haste.

Souls know this as a holy land—of stone circles, of poetry and stories that hearken back to pre-history, to when the Tuatha Dé Danann first arrived to claim the island as their own.

Mystery is alive here in sites not entirely of this world where access to finer realms is expected as a usual thing. And artistry's muses work overtime, inspiring poems and songs, paintings and stirring dances that evoke deep communion with the unseen—the natural habitation of the soul who, childlike, romps and plays in fields of wonder until the grown-ups say it's time to leave.

"But not for long," you vow, catching one last glimpse through an airplane window. "I'll be back," you promise, as morning mists and fluffy clouds hide mountains, cliffs and sea from view.

For once Éire has caught you by the heart, you must return to the long-lost love you eventually discover as your soul—who peeks out easily when you're relaxed in a setting that's more like home than where you live.

Ireland's atmosphere feels liminal, delicately hospitable to the soul who prefers candlelight to neon. Indeed, for many Éire is a threshold place where only a gossamer veil lies between this world and the next.

Surely I am caught in her net of mystery. For poetry is my soul's song, and the verses that emerge as I nestle in the island's emerald bosom carry an essence of my true Self that resonates with my Irish ancestors who left here generations ago.

Perhaps the diaspora is returning, called by an ancient longing for reunion that affects all souls, though none so poignantly as those of the Irish. We know ourselves as people of this fair country and we feel its messages profoundly. For the landscape here is a seanchaí with stories to tell and secrets to share.

Lend your ear, and I'll let you in on some of them.

Cheryl Lafferty Eckl

Touching the Timeless in Éire's Ancient East

*May your heart carry you
back to commune with ages past,
long-sheltered in misty happenings
only sacred stones recall.*

Wonders

What did the builders of Newgrange
call their masterful creation?
Womb of the Mother?
Sacred vessel of Earth's treasures?
Blessed house of life and harvest?

Step inside and feel the presence
of deep conviction
and faith in seasons turning
brought about each winter
when Solstice sun
runs straight down the passageway
that never was a tomb or house of the dead,
despite symbolic ashes in side basins.

Only vitality shines here to bring again
fertility and springtime blooms
planted in the darkest dark
as seeds must be
else they will not see the light of day
come Imbolc and Bealtaine.

Triple spirals mark the portal,
as sentinel stones keep watch
telling all who cross this threshold
that mystery abides within.

What transpired is long since lost,
buried in green Éire's lore and soil
whose memory would speak to those
whose ears are willing to be quickened.

Listen when the lights go out.
Do chants of Old Ones whisper,
beckoning you to pray once more
for new blessings from the land?

Five thousand years is not too long
for their voices to still echo
down monumental corridors
of wonder.

I marvel as I walk away—
how could mere farmers moving rocks
build on such a massive scale
to mind the Earth
as she kept them and their families
nourished body, mind and soul
high atop the River Boyne?

On Tara's Hill

Raindrops fall on Tara's Hill
like saint's tears cleansing the high ground
where angels may have first touched down
to make their earthly sojourns
in a land so lush
that they believed
it could only be another heaven.

Approach the hill with reverence
as did the Old Ones who prayed here,
their rituals hidden in memories
of Druids and local royals
who buried their dead and honored them
in mounds as old as Brú na Bóinne.

Let your mind go deep within.
Your soul knows how to plumb the depths
of ancient Éire's history
that lies beneath this grassy hill,
all the way to limestone beds
that hold the secrets of the land
and her people's identity
that is not separate from this soil.

Stand on Tara's earth awhile.
One feels a prestigious power,
as of a dwelling place for gods

who traveled to the Otherworld
from wells and thin places now lost.

No wonder warrior kings of old
fashioned ring forts on the hill,
claiming the summit as their domain,
calling it Teamhair na Rí,
creating legends to prove their rights.

Though Patrick felt a foreigner
amongst the country Celts he served,
his faith kept faith with their beliefs,
traded them a Son for Sun,
and let the land speak for them all
in rituals and festivals
that marked the seasons holy turnings
of sowing, growing,
death and rebirth.

Tara holds dichotomies
from the past and of today
gently in her mystic heart
and welcomes all to pledge their troth
to her lineage of communion
'twixt hungry souls of every ken
who know themselves as Éire's own.

Stepping Through Time in Dublin

Let your feet decide
    where walking should take you.

Across St. Stephen's Green
    past its glorious central fountains
    and ponds alive with ducks
    who see no reason for migration.

Why travel from Paradise
    when on the borders of this verdant refuge
    all manner of human and divine delights
    beckon the pilgrim to welcome silence
    and wait for inspiration.

And come it will.

Go early to Trinity College
    to see the Book of Kells and marvel
    with eyes wide open in amazement
    at what devoted minds and hands
    created to last a thousand years.

Vikings and Old Irish walked here
    and built and fought and carved a city
    out of sea and river and land that yielded
    to mankind's determination
    to make their mark.

So astonished to be alive
	they had to leave a legacy
	to prove the truth of their existence
	in books and monuments
	in waterways and bridges
	in parks and shops
	and in St. Patrick's magnificent cathedral.

Everywhere I walked today
	I saw evidence of a genius spark
	that would not be silenced or held back
	(no matter the century or scenery)
	of people who claimed their right
	to make a life in Dubh Linn.

In the Presence of the Goddess Brigid

Sitting in the dark,
her sheltering arms around me,
I rest my ear upon her breast
and hear beating there
the rhythm of eternity—
compassion in three-quarter time,
waltzing in the joy of conversation,
the sharing of transcendence
I know she wants for me.

A goddess's heart is a listening organ,
a portal of generous welcome
that hears my soul's unconscious prayer
for her acceptance and her blessing.

She answered before I asked.
Only I must grant myself permission
to nestle into helplessness,
to slip into the blue ocean of her silence
where my every in-breath comes
from her exhaled affection.

Am I the only one who did not know
her attentive heart
has always been a presence
that sustains me?

Rest, my child, she says, you're safe.
No matter where you walk,
    you are never lost to me.

Match your being with my own.
I know your gypsy rhythms
    and love you for them;
for, like medieval Irish bards,
    you shine brightest in the dark.

Be still and you will find me there,
my mantle ready to enfold you.
Come, tarry here beside my fire
    and tell me all your poems;
I do delight in them and you.

Believe that now for all our sakes.
Beauty is the reason.

Holy Ground

Saint Kevin's presence brightly shone
upon that July afternoon,
warmer than all other days,
welcoming us pilgrims back to his fold,
we, who remember his embrace.

He surely smiled at my salmon lunch,
not as simple as the fish
an otter brought to feed his monks
after Kevin's recluse years
when word spread of his sanctity
and crowds of followers begged of him
to leave the shelter of his cave
and work his miracles for them.

Avowed ascetic though he was,
he took advice of his friend Ciarán,
saintly founder of Clonmacnoise,
and began his own monastery,
realizing this sacrifice
as another way to God—
withdrawal working in its season,
not more or less, as Christ found out
when duty called him from the desert.

So Kevin laid his hermit heart
upon the altar of his church
and pilgrims came to him instead,
basking in his light that stayed,
heedless of the woes of time.

A stone arch gateway leads the way
across a bridge to Kevin's world,
sanctified by the man himself
whose hand stretched out
in raptured prayer
once gently held a blackbird's egg
until the baby chick was hatched.

I knew then on that July day
how the little birdie felt,
nested in the saint's warm palm
as if the hand of God himself
held me in his surety,
safe to stay, to test my wings
before trying out the breeze
that would carry me away.

The Sally Gap was our way home
through Wicklow Mountains'
twilight mists.
A soft rain fell like Kevin's care.
And when a rainbow came in view
I felt it as a miracle,
a sign of promises fulfilled
by saints and angels who abide
on holy ground at Glendalough.

Living Full Soul
in County Clare

May you come alive with the sound
of landscape speaking profoundly
in the silence of distant valleys
& the roar of waves crashing
on primordial cliffs.

First Glimpse of The Burren

Set adrift from the motherland
Like a lone calf
Out in the sea she floats
Haunted home of the ancient ones
Who, generations ago,
Pushed against the nature gods
And claimed the land
As their own

Only to be claimed themselves
By salty wind and grey-blue sky

And turned into the very stone
That would not yield to tyrants
But that settled into line
Under the spell of the
Wall builder's imagination.

In Relation to Silence

You've never heard a thing
Till you've stopped on a mountain
That's all cracks and hollows
And listened to the sound
Of your own suspicion
That you would not find your way.

You've never listened in your life
Like you did today—
Desperate for a prompting,
A sign of the passage through,
Only to stumble into the miracle
Of a fellow traveler's helping hand.

Your well-tuned heart
Brought you to this place.

Now listen for a new song
Playing in the silence
Of unpeopled landscape,
And know yourself as eternally
Minded by the immensity
Of your own life.

Ancestral Home
(in honor of John O'Donohue)

Not long ago this dry stone cottage,
now overgrown with tree and vine,
shielded parents, children, animals
all surviving
perhaps even thriving
when song and Spirit visited.

Their eldest son became a priest,
honoring his parents' prayer for blessing
upon their lineage that held little else
to distinguish them from others
feeding their loved ones from the land.

Times were hard for their ancestors,
made harder still by foreign foes
who scourged the people,
a common act of occupiers
who did their worst in Ireland's past
to bind the stubborn Celtic soul
that knows its natural state is free.

Yet in this home good will prevailed
in art and verse and stories told
of human desire for belonging,
of conversation 'twixt land and sea,
of unfettered imagination
and of connection with the essence
of one's deepest, soulful self.

For that is what the young man found
in kinship with primeval landscape,
in vast horizons of stone and sky
and wild blue waters beckoning him
to distant shores.

In chapel ruins
where courageous priests
said mass in secret
and prayed like Saint Coleman
alone in his cave for seven years.

And in the somber face of Christ
hewn in stone by Nature's hands
hidden in a far valley
soft with grasses
and wildflower fields.

Here in sheltered inspiration
poets, pilgrims and fond dreamers
come to honor the lovely man,
too soon departed,
yet still alive in each shared pathway,
in seasons cycles of eternal change
and in the wise Celt's knowing
that soul and soil
still need each other,
even in a modern age.

Hearth Fires
(for the Lads)

Hearth—a gentle word for heart of the home.

Lift up your soul and be gathered in
By a turf fire's earthy aroma
Blessing your cottage with sheltering warmth
Made centuries ago for this very moment
To ease your body and mind your heart.

Stir again music played full soul
And sung as sean nós at twilight.
Fill your lungs with airs of joy
To chase away old dark night's gloom.
Nature made this fire for you.

Ignite a spark in the home of your heart.
Cast your glow out on the land
Like a glorious sunset.
The whole world is your Irish cottage.
Be the flame to bring friends in.

May you become the hub of a wheel
In whose presence others stay
For guidance, grace and fellowship
Until each one should leave this nest
To garner their own nucleus.

You're meant to be like a fiery core
With many or a few chosen spokes,
Depending on your steadfastness
In the center of your wheel.

Yet, oh, how rough a task it is
To round off stubborn square corners
So you can spin or spiral or turn,
Encouraging others to ascend.

The answer lies in your heart's home
Where you become a whirling flame
In the midst of those cherished ones
The Universe would draw to you.

Kindle that warmth and you will see
How Spirit in you does it best.

Igniting Creativity at Kenmare

May your imagination leap & twirl,
forging novel pathways to the
sun & moon & stars;
they entertain no limitation.

At the Writers Retreat

Bealtaine's fires burn double
To purge old winter's dark
And light the way to springtime's green
Where Imbolc's three-month lambs frolic
And May Day's festivals mark
Exuberant new life for young and old.

Inspiration sparks afresh,
Each view across the bay or estuary
An invitation to plant seeds of thought
In imagination's fertile ground,
To raise up word flowers
Waving their bright-hued blooms
For attention from passersby
Whose hearts they hope to gladden.

Creative fires burn bright at Parknasilla,
Fed by geniuses who loved the place,
Leaned into its fecund quiet
Until Nature's luxuriant empathy
Filled them with such passionate insight
The only way to live was to write
Till they were empty vessels
Begging to be filled again.

So were we also sparked,
Ignited by a bardic spirit,
Nourished by the pleasing
Sound of pen on paper,

Urged to freely splash
In creation's risky tributaries,
Until we, too, should find a seat
In the company of literary mightiness,
If even for one precious moment,
One brilliant phrase of prose or rhyme
That flashes into the mind like lightning

A gift from the word gods who live on,
Beside the waters of Kenmare Bay.

Liminal Flame

Scratch the match.
The instant before spark
flames to fire,
one hand holds the surface,
one hand strikes the stick.

We count on the sound
to confirm our intention
to light, to burn,
to warm or to consume.

Do we ever know for certain
before the flame is kindled?

Will the flame rise
if we do not strike?

Or does it already exist
in the mind and the heart,
needing only the hand
to confirm what the soul
has known all along—

that Spirit's fire is eternal,
ever-present, yet absent
unless we strike
the match of consciousness.

The unseen needs the seen
to prove the reality
of the conversation
that feeds the flame—

the fire begun
in the imagination
and stoked full blaze
when we reach through the veil,
and with a willing heart and hand
grasp Eternity's fire
and bring it home
to do its work.

Along the Faery Trail

You need not be a child
To enjoy a stroll on the Faery Trail,
Though child eyes are useful
For noticing with wonder and delight
The tiny houses grown-ups built,
Perhaps to recall the faery forts
Their own parents dubbed imaginary,
But as children they knew were real
Because the faeries let them see.

Child eyes turn from the path
And peer through gnarled branches,
Soft tufts of long grass,
Vines and rhododendron trees,
Spying openings into cozy spaces
That have the feel of real faery dwellings,
Their private homes—
Those not designed for viewing
By doubters of their presence.

What if we took away decoy houses
And still named the path Faery Trail?
Who would observe and what would they see?

My soul leaps up to play the game.
Who knew child eyes could reawake?
Such is the touch of faery magic,
No matter how old you think you are.

From Darkness to Light

Robin woke in the dark,
feathers all aflutter
in coming out of rest.

She fluffed her body,
bringing fresh air into her lungs
and under her wings
as she stretched on the branch
where she had sheltered in sleep.

Gathering all her energy,
she lifted up,
letting the wind
that stirred the tree
carry her to a higher limb
where she let out the first notes
she knew the Sun depended on
to begin its journey across the sky.

Puffing out her ruby chest,
Robin reassured herself—

"My job is to remind the Sun
to shine its warmth upon the Earth.
If I do not sing today,
the world will surely petrify
remaining forever
in cold darkness."

She was not entirely certain
of the absolute truth
of her belief,
but she was not willing
to test its accuracy
by withholding her song
from even a single day.

The longer the nights of winter,
the more difficult the dawn
on stormy mornings,
the more exuberantly Robin sang.

She trilled, she twittered,
she varied the notes,
not limiting herself
to what others might consider
sufficient unto the day.

The fewer the light hours,
the more fiercely
she called to the Sun
until she felt it answer.

Some dawns whispered into being
with gentle mauves and blues,
brightening only
into the misty greys of a soft day.

Others answered her call
with glorious beams of gold,
orange, ruby and purple.

And then—pure ecstasy!
The Sun's bright response
she lived for.

Radiating from below the horizon
the Golden Orb cried out,
"I am here. And shine I will!"

Lost & Found

Just for today, she says to herself,
I'll give myself permission to play
without imposing an agenda.

Setting out her colors, aligned, just so,
she opens a new page in her book,
empty, except for line drawings,
beckoning her to fill them in
with swaths of color, rich and bold
or light and pastel—whatever she likes.

This is for me, she says aloud,
not quite believing she deserves the treat
of whiling away an hour in play.

No worries, she says. This isn't art,
only a silly coloring book.
I don't have to create art.
I just want to amuse myself.

Amazed to feel her hands a-tremble,
choosing crayons over pencils,
surveying the box of waxy markers,
she declares, I need color!

And grasps the most vibrant red,
the deepest blue, the brightest yellow
and the green that calls to her
like every forest she has ever dreamed.

Just do it! she commands her hand
as it falters before the drawing—
a circular mandala design
with window panes that call for gold
and amber lights to brighten the page.

So she begins, gingerly at first,
testing the pressure her hand must use
to make the diamond patterns shimmer
and glow within, as if candle-lit.

Then the green, tracing shapes of leaves
or stems or ovals around the mandala.
None are the same, she lets them change,
relishing the contrast of dark and light.

Now the red—all urgent passion,
demanding its own perfect place
in flower shapes and tiny hearts
that wink out from the inviting circle.

More color! Now! 'Tis time for blue—
and several shades to blend and swirl.
No clash among these myriad tints
when blue is in the calm connections.

She loses herself, at last,
in teal and aqua, sapphire, cerulean—
so many blues that speak to her
of waters, jewels and cloudless heavens.

Each one exudes an energy
of deep communion with her Self
who does not fear or hesitate,
but dives into the colorful flow
that brings her insight more alive.

For now she's also hearing sounds
of blue and red and green and gold
as if they were a symphony—
a singing rainbow of vibrant rays
that pick her up and carry her
straight into a magic world.

And to a portion of her heart
that has lain dormant for so long
the portal is nearly rusted shut.
Color it open! her inner voice begs.
Pick a hue and clear the way!
Unlock the vision that calls to you.

So like a wand her crayon moves
across the page in lightning strokes,
freeing a bright yellow door
where sunlight streams across the threshold.

This is your radiance, her inner voice says.
Embrace it—dip into its glory.
There is only abundance here
and palettes of the possible
waiting for you to paint your life.

See how easily you prime the pump;
get lost in the flow and find your Self
in an hour's simple play.

Create and re-create these hours;
notice how burdens fall away,
problems are solved and joy radiates
in and through and all around you.

You are the art and artist both,
made real by stepping into color.

Dancing on the Threshold at Bealtaine

The fires of change must be tended.
I am beckoned by those flames
to pay attention to their purpose
lest their blessings be for naught.

No need to ponder what's left behind;
even once-loved items are transformed.
I carry inside me things long-cherished
and have no need of outer symbols.

I sit balanced on the threshold
at a point 'twixt here and there.
Clothed in *Yes!* I rise and call
unto distant purple hills.

Yes! I cry and feel my voice
return to me in affirmations
that ripple past on a resolute breeze,
out into a concrete world
that has forgotten what *Yes!* sounds like.

My heart is a drum beating a rhythm
that moves my feet to dance in the Earth
around the fires in a sacred circle,
of weathered stones surrounded in pines.
They all understand the meaning of *Yes!*

If the trees could, they'd pull up their feet
and prance around the circle unrooted,
lifting up their dark green skirts
and waving in grateful ecstasy
while the stones nod appreciatively.

Today I dance for all of us,
rising up tall as the lofty pines,
feeling the Earth beneath my feet,
circling the fire faster and faster
until the flame and I are one.

Leaping, crackling, tossing out sparks
of worn-out ways that are consumed,
I have lost all names but *Yes!*
And knowing the truth of my eternal fire,
I cross the threshold of Bealtaine
and dive into the flame of the dance.

Departure
(at the end of a writers retreat)

Home beckons now,
    the one you care for differently from
    the faery land from which you must depart.

Every mountain-top ascent
    requires a coming down.

Even masters of great wisdom
    often descended to extraordinary depths
    before they finally lifted off
    to that bright world: the Isle of Promise,
    blest Tír na n'Óg, the Land of Ever-Living.

Not yet, not yet!

May we not stay yet a moment longer
    to share the Noble Call, a parting glass
    with friends of old and new,
    our precious gathering of mystics.

Travelers we have been together,
    pilgrims on word journeys too rare
    and holy to ever speak of entirely to those
    whose eyes have not beheld the Skellig,
    whose feet have not walked
    in rhododendron corridors,
    who have not bridged the moon
    and ruby fire reflected in still waters.

For to tell too much of Bealtaine
    is to scatter sparks of mystery
    that are better tucked away
    like a pink rock hidden in your pocket
    where no one else can see
    the reason for your smile
    when fingers touch the talisman
    and transformation comes again
    in twin fires of recollection.

My friends! O, my friends!

May your days find ease
    and banquets of joy spread out before you
    through ten more ways into your truth
    of vivid words and observations,
    portals into timelessness—
    that place where we may meet again
    as Parknasilla's hospitality continues
    to unfold according to its seasons.

Bathed in the Shannon's Holy Waters

*May you take your ease by river's shores
& ruins still vibrant with devotion
as you feel the tender blessings
of presences who rejoice in your arrival.*

Sunset at Lough Derg
(the River Shannon's largest lake)

Light's essence slipped
behind the mountain
trailing its long train
of golden-orange radiance

blinding the eyes
of those who gaze too long,
winking good-night
but not farewell.

For twilight's glow
promises mornings rosy risings
reflecting pinks and purples
on the placid lake

that welcomes dusks and dawnings
as have come and gone
since the unfailing Sun began
its timeless journey
around our grateful planet.

Following the Muse's Lead

Come sit by still waters, my muse beckons.
Look with the eyes of the Otherworld
and notice what I see.

Slip into your poet-self
and drift with me into dreamtime.
I have metaphors and similes
on my heart today
that I must share with you.

And so I take up journal and pen
and pay attention
to the muse's promptings.

I can only write what is real to me—
as images, events, sensations, sounds
and words that bubble up
from a well-spring of imagination
that is this poet's most cherished gift.

Oftentimes the verses that emerge
feel like holy visitation;
and when I catch a twinkle
in the eye of the Divine,
I am reminded that life on Earth
is a masquerade or play.

We humans are the only ones
who doubt the wisdom
of the Universe's casting.

As a poet, I try not to doubt.
I do my best to play along
and follow when the muse goes
dancing down metaphoric pathways
or swimming in oceans
of word pictures.

Where is your muse leading today?

Listening carefully.
You need not be a poet
to be richly inspired.

The Many Gifts of Dromineer

Cozy cottages nestled together
by the gentle waters of Lough Derg.

Dromineer the village is called.
I do not know the meaning,
except to feel it as a sort of blessing
that brings to life a reminder
to pay attention to the music
of the present moment.

Wake up to holy presences,
to historic shelters
being loved by Nature
into a new form,
for nothing goes to ruin
beside these restful waters.

Rough edges are merely smoothed
by time and dedication to one's calling
to build, to play, to write, to speak,
to follow Spirit where it leads
alone or in the company of friends
whose souls you've known forever.

Take heed of one another's stories.
Give ear to loves and hurts not spoken;
they may be too deep for words.

Yet souls attuned will feel them all the same,
offering insight and compassion
in the oneness of true listening
that brings healing as on angel wings
that fly in on a lively tune
and take their ease
by candlelight and flames a-kindled
through a bevy of willing hearts.

Antiphon

(written in a quiet van on the way to Lough Gur)

Cease all outer conversation.
Expand your view with softer eyes
as body slips into a state
of peaceful being.

Surrounded by the green of earth
and the pearly grey of morning skies,
highways once foreign
begin to speak
of growing familiarity.

And friends met only days ago
now fit like well-worn shoes:
sturdy companions
for walking a path
both mundane and divine.

Gaze inward now where heart fires glow
and listen for your soul song,
the sound of Spirit's
eternal waves of recognition,
lapping at the shore of your reality:
a conversation begun long ago
in light ages of antiquity.

Here is truth, here is love
that will not leave you comfortless.

For in the harmony of knowing
are you known to self and others
as a spark of fire,
a pool of clearest water,
born reflecting divine to divine:
call and response,
in wordless praise and gratitude.

The Druids of Lough Gur

We turned to each other
and nodded—my friend and I.

The moment our van drove
through the tree tunnel that opened out
onto the historic park and lake,
we could feel them.

The Old Ones who had spoken
their wisdom into the wind
that ruffled stalwart oak branches,
whose shady boughs had made groves
for learning and ceremony.

The rites themselves are long gone,
slipped away into antiquity's
misty past,
but the essence remains,
held fast by invisible arms
that wrapped us in their velvet warmth
as we reverently walked the land
that guards sixty centuries of secrets.

Who were these mighty adepts?

Builders in thatch and wattle,
movers of giant stones,
creators of massive circles

that held their powers
in geometry of earth and sky
no primitive could have mastered.

Not separate from the elements,
they fashioned sacred space
like the open palm of Spirit's hand,
each standing stone a living thing
pulsing with the breath of life,
more subtle than a heartbeat,
yet strong enough to draw us
to the vibration of our healing.

We did not walk alone that day.
Our guides were supernatural,
hosts of generosity,
purveyors of mystic wisdom
that human minds could not perceive.

Only bodies pressed upon rocks and soil
made holy centuries ago
began to resonate with the unity
of circles within circles,
breathing in and out together
in unhurried respiration.

We seeped into one another
and were doubly blessed.

Two Abbeys

Man builds his edifice,
the abbey of hands,
to house his sacred treasures,
organize his thoughts
and shelter wayfarers from life's storms.

Nature creates arbors and gardens
under the brothers' stewardship;
minding not the harshest weather,
standing tall against mighty gales,
proving the resilience of growing things,
surpassing expectations
of countless generations.

For those who are blessed to walk in both,
surely Nature's eternal sanctuary
gladdens the heart as deeply
as icons stored in book or vault.

Both abbeys tend the soul
as Nature grows her flowers,
needing light and love and fertile soil
to work their alchemy
of transformation.

Baptism
(at Inis Cealtra on Lough Derg)

Bathed in holy water from sea and sky
intrepid pilgrims come in open boats
to visit Inis Cealtra's sacred ruins
while hidden presences of angels
and of ancestors attend.

Echoing in Teampall Chaimín
ancient chants bring instant tears
that only inner truth can make
from contact with the deep Unknown
and clearer vision of your Self
found in a healing view of Earth
and promises sealed in sacred stones.

Grace glides swanlike here
amongst the ruins and soft mist,
held in wells and hand-hewn bricks
all rough and mossy now
with age and damp—
neglected, yet still sanctified
by invisible devotees
who waken from their silent slumber
when grateful hearts lift up
spontaneous psalms of praise
to honor them.

Go forth now,
you who have been dedicated
in chapels and on hillsides;
for with each pilgrim step
you belong more to the Divine
and your true Self
than before this crossing over.

May the stillness of Inis Cealtra
rest like a mantle of peace
upon your shoulders
to shield you from uncertainty
or unbelief in the reality of blessing
that descends like gentle rain
into open minds and hearts.

Watch and listen for the signs—
a window has been opened to your soul.

Will you let the Sun
of who you are break through?
There, across the water,
as a new horizon gleams,
beckoning, holding out a friendly hand
as you alight once more
upon the shore of origin,
now transfigured and transformed
by immersion on a holy island.

Reaching Out to
the Wild Atlantic

May you feel the kinship of land & sea
as one reaches for the other
in the passionate embrace
of eternal conversation.

Tost - The Silence You Choose
(at the cliffs of Dún Chaoin in West Kerry)

What inscription will you leave today
on this land of Ireland?
He asked a noble question,
but I could only answer, "None."

I dared not presume to write a word
until I felt it called up through my feet,
each step on vibrant, grassy earth
a confirmation of its "there-ness"
and of mine.

Father and forefathers
who honored their mothers
then left for western shores
rejoiced in my arrival,
as if my finding a balanced, fluid stride
somehow brought them home.

I walked for them today,
lengthening my step like men of the land
who relished the wild Atlantic symphony
of wind and wave,
of sideways rain and rocky cove,
as I have never done till now.

Surrender is the passport
they've been waiting
for me to present—
a simple act once done,
yet monumental until then
for those who have not come to ground.

I thought of Wordsworth
bearing witness to the land,
of seeing and being seen,
and I understood at last
the clay's romantic leaning
toward our bodies
and felt my soul's eternity anchor
in the wonderment of discovery,
as if these mighty cliffs and I
were meeting for the first time.

There's more to write.
The journey is not over.
Yet I will sleep better tonight
knowing that Éire and I are joined
in the supernatural bond
of soles touching earth—
the pilgrim's secret revealed only
to those who walk in their tost.

Herding Sheep on Mount Brandon

Steep green pasture
welcomes all manner of feet—
mine and sheep.

Who is leading and who is herding?
I would be mistaken to think
I am urging rams and ewes ahead,
for sheep know the way
to traverse Brandon's
wide, verdant chest.

Behind us
Three Sisters rise out
of the misty grey sea
under patches of Éire's sudden smiles
illuminating hedgerows and white houses
dotting the Sisters' green skirts
that flow effortlessly
down to the Atlantic's
eternal waters.

While I was gazing
at mystical mountains,
the sheep went their own way
on a path that splits.

They have no need of
straight, white sign posts
to guide them to new pastures.

I do for now,
as I join my friends
who kept climbing
while I stopped
to write these lines.

One day I hope to feel Brandon's call
to navigate his presence
and his dwelling place
with only the compass of my heart.

Today I stay on the well-marked path
and dream of what it must be like
to disappear into the mists,
knowing the land will hold me.

Stepping Back from a Threshold

Some crossings are not yours to make.
Though others get through easily,
the gap for you may be too narrow.
Not a fit, no matter how you wish it
to be otherwise.

Who decided you should try?
Even for a bit of fun,
if you're not called,
the stones will not part,
the window will not open.

Misty portals manifest when hearts are ready.
At least for you that's true.

Your steps cannot be idle,
random or ungrounded—
not in this place
where circled stones
repeat a liminal lullaby
and streams flow fresh
from wild mountain cascades,
singing of goddesses and warriors
disguised today as mossy boulders
frozen on the hillside
in primordial conversation.

Come back now—
though your feet beg to keep on walking
toward the valley's end.

Let the steadfast Earth cradle
your timeless dreams
with images of magic
you could not have seen today.

But ask again tomorrow—
just in case.

Paisean - Passion

The fervor of one's calling.
That's what I felt today at An Díseart
sitting in the former convent chapel,
washed in the light of morning sun
that streamed through
glorious stained-glass windows
infusing this delicate holy space
with colors of such intensity,
of blues and reds and golds and greens,
that one could feel the artist's legacy,
his prayer in glass,
still radiating
like an illuminated manuscript
that transcends even sacred texts
with the essence of devotion
poured into these expressions
of his deepest resonance
with Beauty's way
of being in the world.

A young man who lives his passion
in Éire's poetry of word and song
was singing the lament of a mother's loss
as if her tragedy were his own;
and somehow in the hearing,
in the sharing of such earnestness,
I was transported into bliss.

The fervor of one's calling.
I experienced that sensation
many times this week
in the company of Éire's people:
her poets, painters and musicians,
chefs, engravers and shop owners,
actors, teachers, mothers, fathers,
Gaelic speakers who nourish this land
with the ancient sounds
of their cherished tongue.

I felt my body, mind and soul
suffused with the incense
of each one's mastery
in the exquisite embodiment of their gifts
that permeated the atmosphere
they created by their presence
and the almost childlike delight
that twinkled out
from the smiling eyes
of ones who have become their art,
as they poured the essence of their being
into each pilgrim's receptive heart,
an upturned chalice waiting to be filled
with Beauty's liminal communion.

As I made my way from the
sun-washed chapel
and stepped out into a luminous day,
inspiration shimmered in my heart
as a glimmering sense of purpose—
a phrase I have written before,
now made new in anticipation
of becoming the art
that waves me on,
that bids me live my own life's passion
with the full fervor of my calling,
however Beauty's way
may unfold for me
in the future.

Staying Power

How do you remain when going is not an option,
or has not yet appeared as a call to other shores?

Whose ocean do you long to sail when
yours is still a mountain, and home is
where you're planted by a river, not a sea?

Islands disappear from view
in a cloud's volition, not their own.

You push horizons far away.
What if you sat and let them come to you?

Let the ocean harmonize with the melody
you have yet to learn. Then, and only then,
will the longed-for vision appear to you.

Be the liminal where sky and sea
and sand create each other.

Until you embody the threshold,
your island will remain a mystery.

In the Artist's Garden

Sit on the seat and make a wish.
Close your eyes and trust the promise.

We all lined up to take our turn—
a quick contact
with the artist's stone bench
reputed to have magical powers.

Words failed me.

I seem to be going blank in this place—
as if my mind were always a bit behind
the realizations and forward steps
my soul is busy taking
into my personal island
of passionate simplicity.

Finally, at the path's next turn,
I felt the wish I had not made.

Too deep for words,
the wish made me
in seamless connection
with an immensity
that knows what I'm about.

Fánaí - Wanderer

Pilgrim, voyager,
traveling without an outer place
of house or home.

Inhabitant of worlds not of this one,
permanently impermanent,
following deity's siring
from depth to depth
and height to height.

Ferocious in creation's
ultimate tranquility:
the hurricane's eye
where wholeness is the answer
to what or where or when.

Mission is not a thing,
a timeline or a goal,
a cudgel or a whip
to drive the soul—the tender soul
who longs for kindness and compassion,
space to expand in timelessness
and cozy comfort
to cushion life's rough edges.

As he walks, an inner voice is heard:
Stop here a moment.
Abide with me and learn
the secret of vision in repose.

Look out now across the sea
that glistens in your memory.

Attend with reverence.
Oceans, like dreams,
contain vast motion,
even as they reflect to us
imaginings we have
brought them to be shown.

Take advantage of serenity.
Follow your inner mystery
and your soul will always be at home.

Coming into Unity

Pilgrims with a mutual purpose
were drawn to Ireland to go deep.

Deep into our own glad souls,
into the very soul of Éire,
into her hospitality
that dances between hosts and guests,
givers and receivers both,
blessing all who appreciate
the necessity of one another.

Artists, musicians and our honored chef
came to us or we to them
and joined our hearts in gratitude
that flows from attention paid—
the simple cost of unity.

We understood the grace of giving,
now twice-blessed in the receiving
of a gift from someone's soul;
for then we saw the inner light
illuminating fellow travelers
who shone so bright they dazzled us
and brought tears to our opened eyes.

We traveled up in Spirit's arms
and out for miles upon the Earth,
knit together in Nature's green,
enhanced by tangible devotion
still present in sacred sites of old.

We bonded fast in mutual care,
in generosity both rare and pure
that never failed to swell our hearts
and lost no pilgrim on the way.

Tears were honored, laughter shared
and more eyes were moist
when we took our leave,
knowing our paths
may not cross again,
though Éire's spirit call anew.

What matters is our clear insight
of the divine in one another,
of how each spark was mirrored back
through the gaze of true heart friends
and the joy of one fine dog.

Transformed by Éire

May you come back to your Self
as you gather lost soul bits & bid them
join up like old friends
meeting after a long journey
that no one now remembers.

Soul Retrieval

Attempts are old and pervasive, trying
    to sever the Irish from themselves,
    their culture and their precious land,
    the music of their consciousness,
    the language of their heritage.

Perhaps that's why a rebel spirit
    lives on in hearts that would be free,
    that chafe at foreign occupation
    from thrones and powers near or far.

Éire's soul is in her land;
    she's fought for her identity
    against all odds and centuries
    more consciously than other races
    that have simply disappeared.

Place your feet on Irish soil
    and feel yourself being gathered in,
    as if your soul feels championed here
    by those determined to be seen;
    so that your own soul rises up
    to recognize herself at last.

We Shall All Be Changed

Come walk the beach with me, she said.
Let's stand with our feet in the sea
And let the waves flow rough around us
Until we know the meaning of flow,
Of being remade every moment.

The wind was up at low tide,
Blue, grey, orange, brown, black rocks
Shiny with wet or muted in drying,
Flattened and polished by tidal caresses,
Dotted the damp sand before us.

I looked to my left with some reservation
At vigorous breakers pounding on
Boulders green and mossy.
But she tossed off her shoes and socks
Rolled up her pant legs and waded in
Not waiting for me to come along.

While I dithered, she threw back her head
And laughed into the gusts that blew her hair,
Making her look like some wild Celt warrior
Setting her mind and heart,
Though not against an unseen foe
But in greeting to a lover.

As sunlight waned, the sea felt primal
And she was one with it,
Welcoming each foaming, swirling wave,

As if they belonged together,
Each transforming each into a bit of the other,
In the confidence of mutual affection.

I knew she would not call to me,
But something did—the waves, I think.
A voice I had not heard, until
I watched my friend the sea-lover
Relishing the rhythm of their communion.

The Atlantic was loud, the wind louder,
My reluctance suddenly gone silent
And my heart surprised in listening
To an awareness of courage to trust
In the unseen and step into the Unknown.

She turned only when I stood beside her,
My bare feet tingling in wide-awake attention,
As if the sea had waited for me alone
To teach my mind to believe in the beauty
Of rough waters, the blessing of discomfort.

We shall all be changed, she said,
Gazing far out beyond the cove
That sheltered the beach
Where we both stood, ankle-deep in waves
That no longer felt rough or dangerous.

The question is from what to what.

The Way to Happiness

They danced the music
as they played
fiddle, flute
and Uilleann pipes;

their feet kept time
and begged us join
in the fun
for freedom's sake

to liberate
our fettered souls
and dance away
our reticence,

our fear of living
in the stream
of Spirit's joy
and acceptance

of our imperfect
humanness
that makes us shy
to be ourselves;

when, if we'd dance,
we'd know the truth
of our mutual
awkwardness,

and laugh to think
we'd miss the chance
to let the music
heal our hearts

by starting with
our tapping feet
that know the way
to happiness
flows in Éire
from sole to soul.

Encounter with the Goddess Éire

Preeminent of three sisters,
goddesses of sovereignty,
Éire broods over their island
caring for their children,
bathing them in soft weather
and smiling through the rainbows
that Brigid brought
from heaven millennia ago.

All goddesses have their purpose,
Éire explains from her seat
in the oak grove sanctuary
where she reclines in royal ease.

I personify my people
and infuse my spirit in our land
that none may take it from us.
I live in wholeness
and faithfully strive
to heal their fragmented souls,
unaware as they are
of how lost they appear
from my perspective as a mother.

I embody this threshold place
and hold a portal open wide
for whose willing to step through
into exploration of what might be

when living from the inside out
and daring to touch the point of choice
where decisions tip
one moment to the next.

I negotiate with invaders
and always win the better claim,
for occupiers come and go
while Éire lives eternally—
the creative force making all things new,
imagining novel futures
never seen in quite the form
that they are about to take.

Sovereignty is my intent
for this land and for my people;
they feel my heart and know the force
of my earnest determination
to banish their sense of separation
from the source that enlivens me.

This is the gift I bring to you
and beg you pass the torch along,
sparking hearts who would be free:

Remind them that true self-direction
comes when they live their mystery.

Identity

Poet of soul & fire, she calls herself.
But what does that mean?

She muses.

Stilling her mind, she feels her soul
    nestling into a grounded state
    while her heart reaches starward

    or at least for the housetops
    where she might call out
    the spirited words
    that fill her up with hope
    of touching the hearts of others.

Yet, how, she asks the Universe,
    shall she live in a world
    distracted by its own confusion,

    when all she wants is to disappear
    into the mystery and magic
    of realms not of this plane,

    where miracles are usual
    and the presence
    of unseen helpers
    is to be expected.

For to be a poet of soul
    is to coax the shy,
    tender essence of herself
    to give utterance
    to her most cherished knowings

    to share the rawness
    of her vulnerability,
    and to bear, however briefly,
    the danger of exposure
    she both longs for and avoids.

And, she has come to realize,
    to be a poet of fire
    is to stand in the heat
    of co-creation

    to be chastised by insight,
    consumed by Spirit's intensity,
    ultimately, to be transfigured
    by word alchemy,
    until only her heart remains,
    now purified and made whole.

Bits & Pieces

May Éire's presence
fill your heart & mind & soul
all the days of your life,
no matter the land where you abide.

Gratitude for Those Who Call
(and those who answer)

Éire is for me a pilgrim land. A thin place that beckons my soul across material thresholds to worlds of spirit and imagination.

Each pilgrimage has been in answer to a call from a person, a group and, now I see, from Éire herself—matron goddess whose power and courage gave the land its name and character.

Éire stepped out of the mists as I expressed my gratitude for these poems and for the experiences that inspired them. I should not have been surprised at her appearance—and she told me so. For if you desire visitation from a goddess, speak her name with reverence and thank her for her many gifts.

John O'Donohue

The lineage of my Irish pilgrimages began with philosopher, poet and high priest of Celtic spirituality, John O'Donohue. I never met this lovely man in person, but I have come to know him through his exquisite writing and through his great good friends in and around County Clare where he was the hub of a wheel of souls who cherish, sustain and promote the spirit of Éire.

John was the kindling that sparked a thousand bonfires in the hearts of those who would know this land and who would, in the process, come to know themselves as carriers of an immense inner landscape they might never have imagined.

John Lee & Sister Mary Minehan

Minister, psychologist, philosopher and heart-friend forever, John Lee included me in a small group pilgrimage to sites of Celtic Spirituality. It was on this tour of Éire's Ancient East that I met Mary Minehan of the Brigidine Sisters in Kildare.

Sister Mary had been a long-time friend of John O'Donohue. Like many of his circle, she was still mourning his death from

January 2008. Out of the compassion of her wise Celtic heart that truly experiences the numinous link between this world and the next, she was the vehicle for a miracle of healing from a deep loss I had also suffered in 2008. (http://solasbhride.ie/)

David Whyte
This groundbreaking poet gave me the courage to claim my path as a writer. His books and tour of John O'Donohue's homeland in The Burren opened my heart to the landscape and the possibility of creating soul poetry as a way of life. (www.DavidWhyte.com)

A double blessing of touring with David Whyte is meeting the musical brothers, Owen and Mícheál (Moley) Ó Súilleabháin, and their mother, Dr. Nóirín Ní Riain, who is a gifted sean nós singer, theologican and advocate of listening with "the ear of the heart." (www.theosony.com)

Owen, Mícheál & Nóirín
I love these people! Give them two minutes of your attention and they will sing the spirit of Éire right into your soul in poetry, song, chant and stories.

And they just keep getting better, as I was fortunate to learn on their Turas d'Anam tour of The Golden Vale. As we visited historic sites along the Shannon River, Éire's thin places took me into deeper, more transformational communion with my inner landscape than I had ever ventured. (www.turasdanam.com)

Libby Wagner & Owen Ó Súilleabháin
"Come write in Ireland for Bealtaine!" enthused Owen's e-mail about spending May Day week in County Kerry.

I gasped when I read his invitation. I had just written a scene in my novel about a woman who takes part in a retreat for writers in Ireland. Talk about a sign from the Universe! I had to go!

Owen conducts the Bealtaine retreat with Libby Wagner, a gifted poet and super workshop facilitator. A better team for creating a transformative writing experience is hard to imagine.

Together Libby and Owen shine a bright light into the dark corners of creative uncertainty. And they promise so much fun, you can't help but join them—trusting that because they declare that treasures await in whatever you compose, you will find them. (www.WritingInIreland.com)

Mícheál Ó Súilleabháin (the Elder)

One night during the writing retreat our group was blessed with a special concert by Owen and Moley's father, the late and truly great Mícheál Ó Súilleabháin, accompanied by his wife, Helen Phelan, and their son, Luke.

Experiencing the maestro's musical genius was for me an encounter of a lifetime—an event too magical even for poetry.

Dónall & Pádraig Ó Héalaí & Family

Meeting Dónall, his delightful father, Pádraig, and their generous family of native Irish speakers was like greeting old friends after a very long absence. My heart overflows with love for these fine people and their sweet border collie, Stocaí.

The week I spent with them on the compellingly mystical Dingle Peninsula, immersed in Celtic language, art, folklore and music, was truly a homecoming and a soul gift I will cherish all the days of my life. (www.CelticConsciousness.com)

Masters, Angels, Saints & Celtic Gods

Finally, thank you to St. Brigid, St. Kevin, St. Patrick and the Spirit of Éire herself. This book is for you and all the Irish angels and masters who have guided my path since the first childhood day when I declared to my parents that I knew my soul was Irish.

David at The Burren, 2012, reading from his recently-published book, *Pilgrim*, a few poems dedicated to the memory of his friend John O'Donohue.

My favorite picture of Nóirín, from Turas d'Anam, 2018, clothed in the powerful spiritual mantle she was born to wear.

Libby & Owen, Bealtaine, 2018, relaxing during an afternoon ramble on a beautiful day outside the famous Parknasilla Hotel in County Kerry.

Moley & me, Turas d'Anam, September 2018. Now that he's fully embodying his poet's voice, I have to call him Mícheál. Here we are, celebrating each other's latest verses at Dromineer.

Dónall & Pádraig, son & father, in May 2018, welcoming their first guests to the Celtic Consciousness tour of Pádraig's homeland, the Dingle Peninsula.

Nóirín, Cheryl & Owen, Turas d'Anam, September 2018, after a mountain hike, with the Shannon River in the distance below us, before the rains came.

About the Photos

Cover photo: Three Sisters peaks as seen from the ring forts at Ceathair Deargáin on the dramatic Dingle Peninsula. In Celtic lore these hills represent triune goddesses, Ériu, Banba and Fódla, who attempted to prevent the Milesians from conquering their island home.

Pg viii: My dream of an Irish cottage; privately owned. I could have moved right in, except for the folks who already did.

Pg 2: Entrance to Newgrange, a 5,000-year-old structure oddly called a passage tomb. More likely a site of ritual, the top opening is perfectly aligned so the winter solstice sun beams a shaft of light down the 60-foot central passage to illumine the main altar at the back.

Pg 5: The River Boyne. Located in the area of County Meath known as Brú na Bóinne which contains over ninety Neolithic monuments.

Pg 12: Crossing to the monastery at Glendalough, founded in the 6th century by St. Kevin and still a popular pilgrimage site. Most remaining buildings date between the 10th and 12th centuries.

Pg 16: Dry stone wall at sunset in The Burren. Evidence of the skill of builders who understand stone as a living thing.

Pg 18: The Burren looking toward Galway Bay. These hills were once covered in forest. When the trees were gone, rainwater washed away the soil, leaving this astonishing limestone landscape that supports a diverse ecosystem of plant and animal life.

Pg 22: Known to many as "the Lads," Owen and Mícheál (Moley) Ó Súilleabháin are multi-talented, Irishborn singers, composers, instrumentalists, poets and passionate custodians of Celtic word and song. Photo courtesy of my friend and fellow lover of Ireland, Patricia Brigid Byrne-George.

Pg 26: One of many cozy fires I enjoyed in Ireland. The cool, damp climate welcomes a hearty blaze most any time of year.

Pg 29: A view of Kenmare Bay taken from the vast property belonging to the Parknasilla Resort. Sometimes you can catch a glimpse of seals sunning themselves on rocks in the distance. Catching sight of the resident faeries is more of a challenge.

Pg 32: A winsome cottage hidden along Parknasilla's Faery Trail for the delight of children young and old.

Pg 43: Known as "The Druid's Circle" in Kenmare, southwestern County Kerry. The day I visited this magical place, the pine trees were waving in the breeze like Druids dancing.

Pg 44: Full moon at Bealtaine (April 30 - May 1) shining on the wetlands of Kenmare Bay. I took this photo on a rustic bridge at twilight with a spectacular ruby-fire sunset behind me.

Pg 48: Driving north along the Shannon, about halfway up Lough Derg lies the village of Dromineer with its tidy marina, park and Waterside Cottages. A perfect place for enjoying a restful holiday and inspiring views across the water.

Pg 58: Long considered a symbol for the soul, this lovely swan welcomed my friends and me to Glenstal Abbey, a Benedictine monastery and school where guests may also find surcease from the burdens of modern life.

Pg 60: Ruins of the Romanesque church of St. Brigid on Inis Cealtra (Holy Island). The only access to the island is by open boat. The original monastery was built here in the 7th century. Holiness still abides in this place.

Pg 64: Cliffs at Dún Chaoin on the Dingle Peninsula, the furthest western point of Europe. The primordial energy of earth and sea colliding along this rugged coast is breathtaking.

Pg 69: These are the sheep I stopped on Mount Brandon to write about. Their wooly bodies dot the landscape from every view.

Pg 72: An exquisite chapel at the former convent of An Díseart, which is now a vibrant center of Celtic spirituality, culture and pilgrimage in the heart of Gaelic-speaking West Kerry. The center has a special interest in beauty and art from a spiritual perspective. (www.diseart.ie)

Pg 78: One of many day-hikers who make their way up Mount Brandon. For some, the climb is sufficient in itself. To others, walking this path becomes a profound pilgrimage on a trail of saints protected by Brendan the Navigator.

Pg 84: I decided to sit at Ventry Beach while others went walking along the three-mile strand. Ireland never disappoints when you stop and let your gaze expand.

Pg 86: Clogher Beach at day's end after deep communion with the living, breathing elements of earth, sea and sky.

Pg 91: Our very own céilí in a wonderful old cottage. A céilí is a delightful gathering of friends and neighbors for food, fun and fantastic traditional music. Provided here by the duo Kern on pipes and fiddle; Aoife Granville on flute. Not shown, Gerry O'Beirn on guitar; vocals by Eliís Ní Chinnéide.

Pg 92: Tapestry of the Goddess Brigid bringing rainbow light to Éire. Photo taken at the Solas Bhríde pilgrim center in Kildare.

Pg 98: Another photo of Clogher Beach. These scenes of waves crashing onto rocks are one of the reasons the Dingle Peninsula is such a mesmerizing place to visit.

Pg. 102 - 103: Scrapbook pictures for a bit of fun with my beloved Irish friends. The lovely photo of Nóirín is courtesy of Patricia Brigid Byrne-George.

Pg 108: A different perspective of Ceathair Deargáin. The family that lived here centuries ago enjoyed an unobstructed view of land and sea and sky. Looking at this photo, I can almost feel them sending gratitude to the many spirit presences who watched over them.

Mystical poetess Cheryl Lafferty Eckl's love for Ireland began as a child and has only grown stronger as she's spent time there with the land, the people and their goddess, Éire, who gave her name to the Emerald Isle.

In publishing *Sparks of Celtic Mystery*, Cheryl is fulfilling a dream of sharing her deep affection for Celtic culture with fellow travelers and with those who hold a fond place in their hearts for this misty isle that invites exploration of inner and outer landscapes.

Watch and listen to more of Cheryl's poetry, and learn about her other books, blog and extensive library of articles on her website at www.CherylEckl.com.